Cheesecake for Shavuot

This **PJ BOOK** belongs to

_____

_____

pj Library®

JEWISH BEDTIME STORIES and SONGS

By Allison Ofanansky
Photos by Eliyahu Alpern

KAR-BEN
PUBLISHING

To all the kids in this book—wishing you a lifetime of abundance and sweetness.
To my husband Shmuel—couldn't do it without you (and wouldn't want to) and to my
parents for all their love and support.
Thanks to the Center for Healthy Living in Tzfat (www.halevav.org) and the Matnas
Sekter community center for providing the garden space.
— A.O.

To my sons, Yagel and Nitzan: May there always be lots of goat cheese in your future –
hopefully from your own goats – and may you have your own farms one day.
— E.A.

Kar-Ben Publishing
A division of Lerner Publishing Group, Inc.
241 First Avenue North
Minneapolis, MN 55401 U.S.A.
1-800-4-KARBEN

Website address: www.karben.com

Library of Congress Cataloging-in-Publication Data

Ofanansky, Allison.
    Cheesecake for Shavuot / by Allison Ofanansky ; photographed by Eliyahu Alpern.
      p.   cm.
    Summary: Students in Israel plant wheat in the fall, watch it grow during the winter, and harvest it in
the spring, threshing, winnowing, and grinding it until they have flour which, with cheese from petting
zoo goats and strawberries they have grown, will make their Shavuot dessert. Includes a cheesecake
recipe.
    ISBN 978–0–7613–8126–6 (lib. bdg. : alk. paper)
    [1. Wheat—Fiction. 2. Shavuot—Fiction. 3. Jews—Israel—Fiction. 4. Israel—Fiction.] I. Alpern,
Eliyahu, ill. II. Title. III. Title: Cheesecake for Shavuot.
PZ7.O31Che 2013
[E]—dc22   2012009495

PJ Library Edition ISBN 978-1-5415-3599-2

Manufactured in Hong Kong
1-44966-35814-10/25/2017

051830.3K1/B1205/A7

Today we are planting wheat in our school garden. Nili, our teacher, tells us that in Israel we plant it in the autumn, so it can be watered by the winter rains.

Shoshana and Naomi dig up the earth. We mix in compost, scatter the seeds, and cover them up. Then we give them a big drink of water.

A few weeks later, tiny green shoots appear. "It looks like grass," says Ruth.

All winter we watch the wheat grow.

Just before Passover, Nili shows us that the wheat is making seed heads. Each stalk has two little rows of green seeds at the top.

"Can we cut it and make it into flour?" Leah asks.

"Not yet," answers Nili. "The grains have to ripen. It won't be ready until later in the spring, around Shavuot. That is why Shavuot is also called *Hag Hakatzir*, the holiday of the grain harvest."

As the weather gets warmer and drier, the grain ripens. The seed heads turn brown and droop toward the ground. Finally it is harvest time. Each of us gets a turn to use the sickle. As I cut my stalks, a few grains fall on the ground.

"These are called gleanings," says Aviya. "We're supposed to leave them for the poor, like we read about in the *Book of Ruth*."

"But what poor people are going to come to our school to pick them up?" I protest. "They'll be wasted."

"I have an idea," says Aviya. "We can bring them to the goats at the petting zoo."

When we finish cutting all the stalks, Nili tells us we must leave them to dry in the sun.

We tie them into a bundle called a sheaf and stand it on end. The wheat bends all around, like a little umbrella.

The next day, we take the gleanings to the petting zoo. The goats' tongues tickle our hands as we feed them. Amir, who takes care of the animals, lets us help milk the mother goats. "There is lots of milk this time of year," he says, "because the baby goats are old enough to eat other foods. They will enjoy the grain you brought."

We take turns milking. Itai squirts warm milk into a bucket.

Afterwards, Amir gives us some fresh goat cheese to take home. "With your wheat and my cheese, you can make a cheesecake for Shavuot," he says.

"There are strawberries in the school garden," Ruth adds. "We can make strawberry cheesecake!"

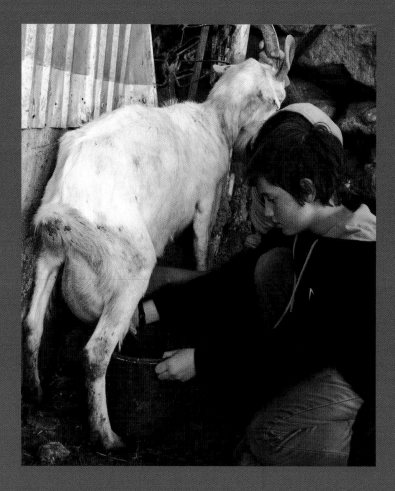

A week before Shavuot the wheat is completely dry. Nili takes apart the sheaf and gives us each a small bundle. We beat the stalks against a tarp and hit them with a stick. The grains fall to the ground. "This is called threshing," Nili tells us.

"There are still bits of chaff and straw mixed in with the wheat grains," said Nili. "The breeze will help to blow them away."

As we pour the wheat from one bucket into another, the wind takes away the lighter pieces of chaff and straw. This is called winnowing. We winnow until only grains of wheat are left in the bucket.

The next day Nili sets up a flour grinder in the classroom. Everyone has a chance to turn the handle. It's hard work. As the grains are crushed between two stone plates, a small stream of flour sifts down into the bowl.

"Now we can make our cheesecake," says Nili.

Naomi beats the cheese with eggs to make the filling.

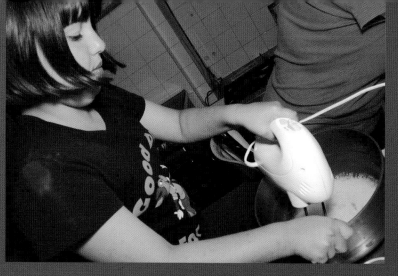

Aviya squeezes in some lemon juice.

Ben adds the vanilla.

Then we use our ground wheat to make the crust.
Ben mixes in butter and a little water.

Itai kneads the dough
into a ball.

I roll out the crust with a
rolling pin.

Nili pours the filling into the crust and the cake is

While the cake is baking, Chaim and Ruth slice strawberries to decorate the top. Finally our cheesecake is ready to eat. The result of all our hard work tastes delicious.